VOICE OF SUICIDE

VOICE
of
HOPE

VOICE OF SUICIDE

VOICE
of
HOPE

A Mother and Son Speak

Through The Silence

KATHY TRIPCONY

Voice of Suicide, Voice of Hope:
A Mother and Son Speak Through the Silence
Published by Proclamation Publishing LLC
Timnath, CO

Library of Congress Control Number: 2017944975
ISBN: 978-0-692-87729-6

FAMILY & RELATIONSHIPS / Death, Grief, Bereavement
BODY, MIND & SPIRIT / Healing / Prayer & Spiritual

Unless otherwise indicated, all Scripture quotations are taken from the Holy Bible New International Version Copyright © 1973, 1978, 1984 International Bible Society. Used by permission of Zondervan Bible Publishers.

QUANTITY PURCHASES: Schools, companies, professional groups, clubs, and other organizations may qualify for special terms when ordering quantities of this title. For information, email kteechur@gmail.com.

This book is printed in the United States of America.

Proclamation
PUBLISHING

Dedicated to the loving memory of our son, Tim,
whose storms in life overcame him at age 36,
but who is now victorious in his heavenly home
with his Savior.

Contents

ACKNOWLEDGMENTS

IRST AND FOREMOST, I WISH TO EXPRESS
my deepest gratitude to my Lord and Savior, Jesus
Christ, who has held my hand through every moment of my
life and has breathed for me when no breath would come.
Thankfulness to:My hero, encourager, computer guru, rock,
and love of my life, Denny.My compassionate, strong, brilliant, supportive daughter and her family.My faith-filled
sister Ruth, brother Ted, and their families.My Bookies
"sisters," who held me up when I had no strength of my

own. My Cubby Comfort Dog Team, who have journeyed with me through the jungle of grief and healing. Shay Black and Robin Francis, who bravely gave voice to their sons' stories and have spoken hope and enlightenment to many, so others may be helped. Polly Letofsky and the My Word Publishing team: Bobby Haas, editor; Micah Pilkington, Proof Editor; Victoria Wolf, book cover designer; and Andrea Costantine, layout; who courageously took on this book project and made it happen.

FOREWORD

ANYONE WHO HAS EVER LOST A LOVED
one to suicide, or anyone who works with people and
wants to share the mercy and compassion of Jesus Christ
with them – and better understand everything that is going on in a person who is contemplating suicide – This is
a MUST READ book! Kathy writes from a first person
perspective and provides personal insight.

Tim Hetzner – *President / CEO*
Lutheran Church Charities Home of the K-9
Comfort Dogs and Kare-9 Military Dogs
3020 Milwaukee Ave, Northbrook, IL 60062

PROLOGUE

LISTEN. YOU MAY HEAR THE SOFT VOICE
of a loved one crying out because the world is just
too much to deal with. Or perhaps a close friend whis-
pering that circumstances are overwhelming for her right
now. Listen. Bullying at school makes your child feel he
can't face another day in his classroom. Can you hear the
anguish in their voices? They're speaking to us, but we need
to be there to listen. And care. And maybe even find some
help. This book is for all those in our lives who are reaching

out, but don't know how to ask. They need relief, but don't know where to find it.

This book is for all the precious Tims in our lives who are our sons, daughters, coworkers, military personnel, veterans, and friends with whom you share coffee. A brother, father, spouse. This book is in collaboration with our son, who, at the age of 36, took his life on Mother's Day, 2014.

Tim is my "ghostwriter," if you will, for this book. My co-writer. His words are derived from our close conversations. His heart was aligned to mine in many ways from the time he was conceived to the day he died.

Tim was always a prolific writer. In second grade, he wrote his own book, *Golfer Jim*. He compiled poems with friends in high school. As an adult, he co-authored and published a very technical book titled *X Pages Extension Library, A Step-by-Step Guide to the Next Generation of X Pages Components*. Tim was asked to speak all over the world—England, Belgium, the Netherlands, Germany—due to his expertise in the world of computer applications. He had a way with words. His words, interspersed with mine within this book, will give voice to his mental illness and eventual suicide, which were taboo subjects years ago. I grew up in the 1950s and I don't ever remember anyone dying from suicide. I am fairly certain people did, but no one talked about it. To even say the word would have brought too much pain and shame. Back then people didn't talk about personal, private things like that. Perhaps people feared that talk of suicide might put the idea into another's head. It was shuffled under the rug along with the hope it would just go away.

The statistical reality is that each year nearly three times as many Americans die from suicide than from homicide. More Americans kill themselves than die from breast cancer. In Larimer County, Colorado, where I live, there were an alarming 83 confirmed cases of suicide in 2016. That statistic is more than double the number of people killed in car crashes. That extraordinary rate outpaces most other counties in the state and country. Those numbers include veterans, high school students, the young and the old.

The difficulty in today's world is not that we don't want to talk about suicide; it's that we don't know how. No one taught me what to say to my son when he reached out to me. I had very few tools to help him. I knew very little about where to find help within the mental health community in our town, let alone professionals or organizations in Tim's area. I felt alone and lost trying to get assistance for him, which added to my fear of the outcome. I always hoped that things would work out. The finality of Tim's suicide left me with gut-wrenching guilt because I couldn't help him or save him. Talking about any of this with others was shameful and felt too intense for their ears. I really didn't know where to turn to take the next steps. It is my hope that this book will give you resources, insight into mental illness, and the words to speak about this growing epidemic.

Reach out. There are abundant sources of help. The community is beginning to respond. Faith communities are coming together to bring about discussions and provide opportunities for families to talk. Mental health organizations hold group activities with question-and-answer periods and have opened mental health first aid classes that teach lay people how to assist someone in the early stages of a mental health crisis. Even family physicians view their patients differently, looking at the whole person rather than just physical needs.

There is no longer any reason to remain silent about suicide.

You will notice that this book is divided into sections: Prelude, Interlude, and Postlude. These are musical terms that indicate the beginning, middle, and end. Prelude refers to an introduction that sets the tone and leads to something else. An interlude bridges segments of a piece of music or between events. A postlude is the final chapter or closing phase. In wedding ceremonies or church services, the postlude can be very joyful. I chose these terms because music had a significant impact on

Tim and our family. Music, as our family discovered, is the universal language, a way to communicate and connect through other barriers.

You will hear Tim's voice, both the one who took his own life and the one whose life-song still sings to his family, his friends, and his grace-filled Savior after his death. His voice will combine with mine in a symphony, a melodious choir, with other voices chiming in. Those voices belong to other mothers of sons who took their own lives. They are giving voice to their sons' struggles as well as their joys in life. This melodious symphony is orchestrated by the Master Conductor, who has the power to use these voices to help others and bring awareness of mental health issues and suicide to our communities.

This book is the voice of those crying out, but it's also a book of hope. Many communities are bringing about change that can save lives. Resources at the end of this book can provide help for loved ones or yourself. Because of our experience, our family has found hope in reaching out to others who are also hurting through the Lutheran Church Charities' K-9 Comfort Dog Ministry. A portion of the proceeds from the sale of this book will benefit this compassionate ministry.

Embracing hearts through hope,

Kathy Tripcony

PRELUDE

one

"Hi, I'm Timothy John Tripcony"

HER BREATHING WAS SLOW AND STEADY, her heartbeat strong. She looked at me with eyes of trust, and I blinked away the stinging tears that I didn't want anyone to see. The air in the room was heavy with an antiseptic smell and the lights overhead were painfully bright. I buried my face in her ebony fur and held her little body in my arms for the last time. She laid her small head on my arm and I felt the slowing of her heart. The steady thump, thump and her shallow breath told me Mindy's life was about to end. My precious companion, my run-along-beside-me canine, was breathing her last in my eight-year-old arms. It was more than I could endure at the time.

The vet had given my father and me a choice. Mindy's aging spine had deteriorated, and she was only able to stand if she supported her body by leaning against a wall. We could ask for extraordinary measures to preserve what little life she had left. We could pay for expensive pain medications to ease her discomfort. But what kind of life would that be for her? After Dad and I talked about the alternatives and considered what my mother and older sister would choose (they were at home suffering with the flu), we decided it was time for the vet to administer a euthanizing drug and say goodbye.

I asked if I could hold her during the process since I didn't want her to be far from one of us in her last moments of life. And so, with much compassion from Mindy's doctor, the drug was administered. Her life ended peacefully in my arms.

Her pain ended. Mine began that day. I mourned the loss of Mindy-dog. They say the depth of one's grief is matched by the depth of your love for the one that has gone. I believe that now. For days I cried into my pillow, hoping no one would notice how deeply saddened I was. Our whole family missed her intensely. But I seemed to take it hardest, and I knew that this first, significant loss in my young life would stay with me. My mom once said my sadness revealed my sensitive heart.

I write to you today because I have a lot to say…always did, still do! My sister Joy will tell you that as we were growing up, she would try to talk about her day while we were sitting around the dinner table. But I had so many things to say that she was barely able to get a word in edgewise. Being the second-born in the family, I thought the world revolved around me, so I should have all the attention!

Today I share with you my story, my life-song, because I have hopes that it might help someone else. From the time I was in first grade and saw Joey, who didn't have any friends to play with, I wanted to help those that might have been "underdogs." I knew God gave me a compassionate heart when my dad would ask me to go fishing, but I just couldn't hurt that worm by placing it on a hook. My sensitive heart for all of God's creation is a huge part of who I am. That is what drove my relationships, my work, and my community involvement, and it's how I am remembered to this day by friends and family.

That caring heart of mine began to beat under my mother's own heart. The day I was born, November 28, 1977, became my earthly beginning. But it was only the start of my journey. I looked into my father's eyes that day as he held me and saw his love for me. Every moment of discovery became an adventure, with new vistas to be explored. My world was definitely exciting!

The peach fuzz on my newborn head soon turned to red hair, which became an interesting conversation opener when my parents took me shopping. More and more people commented with delight about my hair; I soon figured out that most people are quite amicable! While shopping at the mall after I had learned the "walking routine," I much preferred strolling with strangers instead of family. They were more interesting! I became a people person, intrigued with each individual I came in contact with.

My vocabulary increased as I grew; I often surprised people with the unusual sayings I came up with. At the age of two, I started my sentences with "actually," and then went on to expound in detail about something. But my real voice was the one that came from my heart—my singing voice. Joy loved to sing around the house, chiming in with the records (vinyl, of course) and cassette tapes our mom put on for us. Mimicking my older sister, I sang right along. Music was in our house all day long, including songs on our piano. We watched Mom play favorites on that instrument and danced to her little ditties in the living room or kitchen. Soon music became the very core of my existence. I would sing from the time I awoke until bedtime, singing my prayers before laying down in the car-shaped bed my parents made for me.

My musical debut was in first grade, when I sang the solo in "Let There Be Peace on Earth" at my church. Using a microphone seemed very comfortable for me, and I truly felt like the song's words might be my theme in life. Echoing the lyrics "let it begin with me," I set out to live those words with conviction.

two

A MOTHER'S THOUGHTS

THE WORD "MOTHER" CARRIES WITH IT many emotions. For me, becoming the mother of two was something that initially seemed impossible. As a young married couple, Denny and I tried to start a family but for years were unable to do so. After much prayer, we felt it was God's will for us to adopt. We submitted the paperwork, and then I awoke one morning convinced I was coming down with a stomach bug. This continued for several weeks until I finally made an appointment with my obstetrician. The "bug" was our first child growing steadily within my womb. Is it any wonder that we named this precious daughter of ours "Joy?"

We loved our little family and delighted in all of Joy's antics and growth. We never imagined that when Joy was only 16 months old, she would become a sister! We bought her a baby doll so she would have her own baby to cradle and rock. When we brought Tim home from the hospital at three days old, Joy wanted nothing to do with the doll. She only wanted to hold her baby brother! The two became like twins, running together in the backyard with Mindy-dog, creating works of art with glue and craft materials sent from Grandma in Indiana, and hiking in the mountains of Colorado while gathering logs for the wood stove in our home. Joy was Tim's pretend teacher; she taught him all the basics he needed to know. She was also Tim's entertainer and turned her pink blanket into a "magic carpet" for Tim, pulling him around on it as fast as she could on the carpet or up the stairs. Playing games together passed many hours when snowstorms made it too blustery to venture outside. Reading together delighted both of them. Being a mother to those two was almost more than my heart could hold. Life was good. God's blessings overflowed. Our little family was secure. What more could all of us want?

three

TIM'S TURN

I LOVED EVERYTHING ABOUT SCHOOL! Preschool was an outlet for me. Saying goodbye to Mom each school day was an invitation to adventure. My friends were so interesting and fun to play with. Everything we learned in the classroom was like opening a birthday present in my mind. I soaked it all in with gusto! I would dance all the way to the car when Mom picked me up. I filled our lunchtime with stories of what happened that day, what I learned, who I played with. There was nothing better in life!

Kindergarten was just as magical. My teacher, Mrs. Krieger, sat down with my mom one day and surprised her. "I feel that your son Timothy might be bored with the material that is presented in the classroom and should perhaps begin sitting in on some first-grade classes, reading and math to be specific. I apologize that this school does not have gifted classes to offer, but your son might be on that spectrum."

After talking it over with my dad and considering the pros and cons, they decided they just wanted me to be a boy and not be pushed. I thought that was a wise decision, but what did I know at age six?

Beginning in first grade, I attended a Lutheran school. Most academics came very easy for me. By second grade my teachers knew I needed more, especially in language arts. They placed me with others who had creative flair for the written word, and our teacher fostered our talents with projects like writing plays and developing poetry.

Life was great. Sports were fun and being part of T-ball, basketball, and soccer teams meant new friends beyond school. My favorite extracurricular, though, was piano. Not the lessons, but its role as the door-opener to the world of music. My teacher got frustrated with me because I improvised on each song she assigned. I'd memorize the notes of the song in my book, then play my own version of it. It was soon evident to her and my parents that I could play by ear. I'd hear a song on the radio and play around with notes on the piano to get the same sounds. It wouldn't take me long to replicate what I remembered from the radio on the keyboard. I could spend hours with my musical friend, creating songs of my own and allowing the notes to get into my heart and soul.

The highlight of my grade school years was acting and performing. When Denver Lutheran High School produced "The Music Man," Paul Von Rentzell, the ambitious director, was looking for a young boy to cast as Winthrop. Paul had seen me do some basic acting at school and in church. He asked me to try out for the part. It was a match! But the amount of rehearsals and performances were a lot to ask of a fifth-grader. As luck would have it, there was a talented singer/actor in sixth grade, Ryan, who also qualified for the role. Together Ryan and I rehearsed for weeks, memorized lines, sang the songs, and finally performed in front of the crowds, taking turns on performance nights. That particular opportunity changed my life, and Ryan became a lifelong friend.

Although grade school was easy, challenges with a particular friend were not. He took frustrations about his home life and struggles with schoolwork out on me. This began early, in first and second grade, and only escalated as the years went on. It occurred at school and on the bus as we headed home. I spoke with my parents about the problem and they went to the principal. Nothing was resolved. At home, we prayed for my bully since we understood that his life was not an easy one. Mom and Dad tried to give me tools to use, like trying to talk out our differences. But nothing seemed to work. I even gave wrong answers on tests to get lower scores so my bully wouldn't be jealous of me. By eighth grade, his attacks were increasing.

While out on the playground that year, I heard the rapid pounding of feet behind me. Turning to the sound, I felt the harsh thrust of his hands on my shoulders, shoving me to the gravel below. Surprise and intense pain registered in my brain as my arm crumbled under me. Even though huge tears filled my eyes, I couldn't let him see me cry. If I went to the teacher to report what happened, I feared Mr. Bully would only retaliate further. So I kept quiet. We had a band concert that evening. Not sure if I could play my trumpet, I wondered if I should just let my parents know. But I was tough! I could play through the pain. I was 13, and I could do this! By the end of the concert, pressing those valves was next to impossible without shooting pain in my arm. My parents noticed, of course. At the end of the concert they drove me to the ER, where x-rays revealed a fracture of my arm.

The "fracture" of my friendship with Mr. Bully also became complete. He was expelled from our school. You'd think I would be relieved. But in my heart, I felt compassion for him. His pain was within. My pain was superficial. Years later, that fracture in our relationship would come full-circle.

four

MOTHER'S PRIDE, MOTHER'S WORRY

WE WATCHED OUR CHILDREN GROW month by month from dependent beings into self-sufficient, caring individuals. Each year brought pride for what was developing within our offspring. Their characters were being molded from circumstances, and their strengths were shining, even in the middle of adversity.

The air filled with excited anticipation, sweaty palms, and nervous stomachs as the members of Denver Lutheran High School's choir awaited their turn to perform at

the Cavalcade Choir competition under talented director Pam Stumpf. The last notes of her backstage warm-
up with the students ended and they gathered on stage.
Awaiting the note from Pam's pitch pipe, her protégés'
eyes widened in shock as they became aware their director had forgotten it! How would they begin their opening
number? At that moment, a note from the bass section
sounded out! Tim, who had perfect pitch, voiced their beginning note. With relief registering on their faces, choir
members sang "O Sifuni Mungu" with renewed enthusi-
asm. A standing ovation at the end of the last note lifted
the choir to an emotional high. Obtaining the top rank-
ing and winning the coveted trophy was a sweet highlight
for the students, their director, and especially for Tim,
who reveled in the value of teamwork.

Tim also played trumpet in the Denver Lutheran
High band. Both choir and band tours to new places in
the United States were delights; Denny often accompa-
nied them as a chaperone.

As parents, we relished going to each high school drama production Joy and Tim were involved with. Painting
scenery in preparation for the performances and obtaining costumes and props remain fun memories. Beyond
the actual performances, my fondest memories were the
cast parties at our home after the shows. The smells of
pizza and popcorn in the house delighted us, and our

family room filled with chatter and laughter until the wee hours of the morning. If it was snowing outside and the roads were treacherous, many of those delightful teens spent the night rather than risking the drive on slippery streets. Some even slept on the pool table! We often realized we could not be more blessed.

During one Christmas break, the snow had fallen generously on the gulleys in our Green Mountain area. Tim felt adventurous and I wanted to join my sophomore son. We hiked with our sleds to the hills near our home. The air was crisp; the snow was pristine for sledding. Tim went down each slope first. I followed after watching him bounce and speed down each hill. We chose various courses, and on the final hill, there was quite a distance from the top to the stream below. "I'll check it out first and see what's at the bottom," Tim offered. Down he went, skimming over the surface of the slick snow. I couldn't see him at the bottom, so I waited for him to yell about his great run. But there was no sound. I waited. My gut wrenched. Something was wrong. I yelled his name. No answer. He was quite a tease; was he waiting down there to surprise me? I quickly raced down the hill to the stream, where I saw him lying face-up, not moving. His sled had hit a huge bump in the hardened snow, causing him to land on the back of his head in the partially-frozen water. He lay motionless. I yelled his name. He didn't respond. I approached and he looked up at me, wondering where he was. I told him we were at the gulleys by our house and asked him if he knew what day it was. He didn't even realize it was Christmas break. I was reluctant to move him, not knowing if he had broken his neck. But if he remained in the stream, the icy-cold water would cover him. I looked around. We were the only people on the hill. Cell phones did not exist in those days. I had to get him out of that freezing stream and to a hospital. Suddenly, at the top of the hill, a woman appeared out of nowhere. She called down that she had seen what happened, and she lived just over the hill. She would call an ambulance. The moments until the emergency crew arrived seemed to go in slow motion. I watched as the paramedics gently placed Tim on a board to protect his neck. They placed a number of blankets around him to warm his soaked body.

At the hospital, CT scans determined that Tim had a concussion with bleeding at the base of his brain. They kept him overnight to watch for any swelling on the brain. That night was uneventful, so we took him home in the morning to recuperate. After days of headaches and lots of rest, he recovered. At first, he struggled with memory recall. That subsided, to the best of our knowledge. Now, looking back on his comments about not being able to remember school before fifth grade makes me wonder.

Did the concussion have a more lasting effect than the doctors realized?

The guilt I felt as a mother who had allowed this injury to happen to my child was heavy. As a parent, the responsibility to protect my offspring was a huge one. I carry that weight with me to this day.

five

WINGS TO FLY

M Y LAST YEAR OF HIGH SCHOOL WAS filled with studies, activities, and bittersweet moments. Playing Daddy Warbucks in our production of "Annie" brought me confidence and an appreciation for hard work. Shaving my curly red locks to look more authentic in the role took a bit of courage. It would grow back. But I saw tears in my mom's eyes when she completed the process and gazed from the thick curls on the floor to my bald head!

I should share with you that I wasn't a run-of-the-mill kid. My friends told me I was quirky, the kind of compliment I loved. I didn't want to be a cookie-cutter replica of so many teens my age. I was my own person with a sense of humor that cracked through the veneer of stuffy traditionalists. My license plate, which read "Glo-worm," expressed the funny, winsome persona I revealed to those who knew me. That name was inspired by the stuffed worm I slept with at an earlier age, which lit up when you squeezed it. How many of my teen friends had a car named after a fuzzy caterpillar?

Music and drama were natural areas of interest for me; running track was a side note. But challenging my body with this new regimen took me to unchartered waters. I pushed myself to do the uncomfortable. The end result was not always a victory or outstanding times, but the training prepared me for the Bolder Boulder, an annual 10k race in Boulder, Colorado that my mom and I ran/walked in May of my senior year.

My dad was supposed to join us, but the April before the race, I received a message during class that my father had had a heart attack and was hospitalized. It was a shocking time for me. I'd assumed that both my parents would be there for me for many years. The days that followed—my father's angioplasty, recovery, and time resting at home—were a blur to me, especially with graduation approaching.

During the ceremony of my graduation I remember being at the podium on stage, looking out at the crowd of proud parents and speaking as the senior class president. I saw the face of my dad, who had been so involved in my early life. I thought how thankful I was to God that Pops was here for this important day in my life and what an influence he had been for me so far.

With high school behind me, I chose to attend Concordia University in Irvine, California. One factor that led to that decision was their choral music program. I wanted to major in music and looked forward to singing with a good choral group. Another factor in my decision was that Joy was already attending Concordia. She was pleased with the academics and spiritual climate on campus. It also didn't hurt that the school was close to the ocean and all the dorms were set up as apartments instead of high-rise buildings full of basic rooms. I spread my wings, and off I flew!

In the heat of August, Joy and I drove off in our Toyota Corolla loaded with all our earthly possessions to new adventures miles away in California. While driving through Las Vegas, we took a chance on one of the games and won the largest stuffed dog we had ever encountered. What luck! Back on the road, Joy noticed the heat gauge registering a hotter temperature each time she glanced at the instrument panel. The heat in the radiator climbed, but we both knew that running the heater at full blast could take the heat away from the engine. Driving with all the windows down while we both tried to lean out and catch the breeze, we literally thought we would die of heat exhaustion. The biggest struggle for me was the giant dog that we had won, which was now sitting on my lap since there was no room for it in the packed car! Somehow, we managed to survive our ordeal and reached cooler temperatures further west. This was definitely a memory that cemented sibling survival stories in our minds.

six

EMPTY NEST

THE WALLS CREAKED, THE BEDROOMS remained clean, the phone was quite silent, and the piano didn't reverberate with the daily lilting of our musical children. We were proud parents and owners of the proverbial empty nest. This home of ours had heard many hours of noisy friends, singing voices, trumpet practices, and impromptu piano concerts of Billy Joel's "And So It Goes" or Paul Simon songs. I welcomed Joy and Tim's independence, but I grieved the silence. This is what you do when you are a parent. Give those baby birds their wings and slowly push them out of the secure nest into the world, hopefully equipping them with the tools and support needed to make it on their own.

In Joy's junior year she thrived academically, striving toward her teaching degree. Her involvement in the choir and hand bells fulfilled her love of music. Going to various congregations in the area with Icthus, a Christian drama group, continued her involvement with acting. Tim was also involved in choir and the drama group.

From Tim's phone calls, we concluded that he was disappointed in the introductory classes he had to take to fulfill his music degree requirements. He became involved in many of the activities and groups on campus, but that took time away from serious studying, which left his grades in shambles. We worried about the outcome.

seven

COLLEGE LIFE

B EING AN INDEPENDENT, OUTSIDE-THE-box kind of thinker, I assumed my music classes at Concordia would expand on what I already knew. I envisioned composing and exploring new avenues in the music world with tools to help me achieve those goals. I was wrong. Music theory drove me bonkers! I was ready to launch my musical interests to new levels, and instead I was grounded. I felt absolutely dejected.

Campus life was exciting, and I became involved in

many areas. But mandatory classes stifled my creativity. I called home, actually crying, on one of my worst days. "Mom, I can't do this anymore. I feel like a failure. I don't know what to do about this. I'm so low." I'm sure she was very concerned, since she was in Colorado and couldn't fix this over the phone. Later I found out that Mom called someone in the office and asked them to check on me—she was that worried.

After a year and a half, the administration asked me to leave. In other words, my grades were in the dumper and I was no longer a candidate for further studies. On Christmas break of my sophomore year, I broke the news to my parents that I wasn't returning to Concordia. They were firm, telling me that if I lived at home again, I would need to find a job right away and help with rent and utilities. I could do that. I just needed some time to find what my future would look like.

INTERLUDE

eight

FULL NEST AGAIN?

WE WELCOMED OUR "BOOMERANG" child back to the nest with certain conditions. He could choose to take classes at any of the local colleges. He also would need to find a job to pay for classes and to help with living expenses, namely room and board.

During the Christmas break after he returned home, Denny invited Tim to go ice fishing in the mountains with him and several co-workers. Ice fishing wasn't one of Tim's favorite things to do, but he agreed to go. One co-worker happened to be Denny's boss at US West. During the fishing experience, this cordial gentleman asked, "Tim, where do you work?" Embarrassed, Tim had to reveal that he had no job. The boss was very gracious and asked, "Would you like to apply for a job as a contractor at US West? However, there's a possibility that your father may be your supervisor." Tim considered this and applied shortly thereafter. He was hired immediately, and Denny became his boss.

This opportunity changed Tim's life, career, and was the impetus for his vast computer experience and knowledge of Lotus Notes, the software application suite. During his first year with US West, the union called a strike. Most of the employees in Tim and Denny's department went on strike. The two of them were asked to hold down the fort, and together they held their department together for weeks while the strike lasted. Tim took it upon himself to develop programs that made tasks more efficient. He and Denny ran their department like a well-oiled machine. Tim learned Lotus Notes rapidly, above and beyond Denny's boss's expectations. His innovative approach to any task he was given made him shine. Many co-workers who worked with Lotus Notes came to Tim for advice.

Years after that experience, both Tim and Denny looked back at working together as the best time of their lives, learning from each other, growing closer as father and son.

nine

CAREER OPPORTUNITIES AND LIFE CHANGES

MY CAREER WAS SOARING! I WAS MAK-
ing the most money I had ever earned. Of course,
working for US West was not in the same ballpark as my
high school job at Chick-fil-A. But it really felt good to
be able to afford my own apartment, sock away some sav-
ings, and even buy my own upright grand piano. That was
a real prize! I researched its origin to approximately 1905.
It was the centerpiece of the small apartment I shared with
a friend from childhood. The large piano had class, with

pillars on each side of its front face. The wood was in good condition, buffing up to a nice sheen when I applied a natural stain to its surface. But the sound! The richness of tones and the solid resonance, especially the bass, brought such pleasure when I touched its keys. The only thing missing was a bench. Pops quickly came to the rescue. He custom-built a bench to match the wood of the piano and provided a hinged lid to hold my sheet music. When I bought this beauty, it was quite out of tune. I could have hired a professional piano tuner, but I jumped at the chance to learn something new. So I bought some tuning tools and a manual and taught myself how to tune my prized instrument. What tone, what songs came out of that cherished piano! I spent hours composing songs and losing myself in the notes. Since the apartment walls were pretty thin, I had to be judicious about what time I played. My neighbors wouldn't appreciate songs I pounded out after midnight.

Music. During this time of my life, my creative outlets were my piano and singing with the Littleton Chorale. My bass voice continued to develop as I learned from more seasoned members of the chorale. Practicing and performing in concerts throughout the year gave me pleasure.

Changes on the horizon, especially with my job at US West, caused me to take a lucrative step up in my career. I uprooted myself from the comforts of Colorado and family and journeyed to Albuquerque, New Mexico to work for an aerospace firm. I moved into an apartment in the foothills of the Sandia Mountains. My taste buds also delighted in this new adventure. I found out those buds loved New Mexico Mexican food! The hotter the better! Oh, yes!

Musical opportunities presented themselves in this new part of the country in the form of a barbershop chorus. New harmonies were introduced to me. New friendships developed from our group, the *New Mexichords*. I even created some new arrangements that we performed at concerts and competitions.

But the highlight of my move to Albuquerque was meeting Nicole. We worked together, and our friendship grew as I got to know this brilliant redhead. She really understood me, my quirkiness, and my detailed descriptions of things. She understood computer language like no other. She also loved music, played the violin, and had a lovely voice.

My very best friend became my wife, and I loved her more than anything I had ever loved in my life. We approached our new life together with realism, knowing how challenging it might be but willing to tackle that life together.

Following new career opportunities, we moved to South Carolina, then North Carolina, and finally settled in Georgia. Our home included our two "children," Wanda, the cat Nicole owned when she was single, and Dewey, a precious long-haired dachshund. Wanda was always our baby—Nicole's baby to begin with. But the addition of Dewey added a new dimension to our lives. He brought love, laughter, and became a third sing-along to our classical music duo. When we both sang along to the *Tuba mirum* of Mozart's *Requiem,* Dewey howled loudly, sometimes in tune! Walks in the park were a delight to all three of us.

The veterinarian's news that our young Dewey had cancer was a blow. We cared for him with love, but the cancer was too much. When he eventually died, the grief was overwhelming. Pets can become like children, as Dewey was for the two of us. My heart was truly broken.

ten

THE SONG IS CHANGING

*M*Y HEART BREAKS WHEN YOUR HEART IS *affected, my son, because your heart grew under my own. How I long to hold that heart and get it beating again. How I wish, as your parent, I could fix it, make it all better, and put a Band-Aid on it as I did with your "owies" when you were little. But I can't, because I'm not God. He is the Healer. I rely on Him.*

Tim continued to soar to heights in his career even we, his parents, did not realize he could achieve. He was asked to speak at Lotus Notes conferences worldwide in places like Belgium, England, and at Lotusphere in Florida. His co-authored technical book, *X Pages Extension Library*, became public, and he held several patents. According to colleagues in his field, he was highly respected for his top knowledge in the world of Lotus Notes. But his calls to us became less frequent. His contact with former friends became less and less. He no longer wanted to be a part of a singing group or chorus. His connections with family were distant. He withdrew more and more. He finally revealed to us that he was suffering from clinical depression.

He posted a video on Facebook about an individual suffering from depression. For the first time, we had some understanding of how he was suffering. We also realized that this must have been going on for years without our knowledge. Depression is a disease within the brain, a chemical imbalance that can't be willed away or treated by just trying to be happy. It's as real and can be as challenging to deal with as a disease like cancer or diabetes.

The life-song of my child is changing. The key of that song changes from a major chord to minor. I feel the loneliness in the notes. I feel the pull of the vortex sucking the life out of me, causing real pain inside the frail body of the mother I used to be. I beg for prayers from my closest friends, the prayer war-riors who are part of the Christian book club I lead. They pray for Tim's well-being, his mental health, and his struggles.

Tim calls with the news of his divorce from Nicole. He relates, "We're still friends. We keep in touch daily. But we are unable to be married." I bleed a little inside for both of them. No, I bleed a lot. I can't tell them enough how sorry I am for them. What can I do? How can I comfort them? I feel so very helpless and wish I could mend this. Denny, the ultimate fix-it man, was powerless to fix this, the most personal of storms. We grieved for our children and their marriage.

Six weeks pass, too long not to hear from our son. His eventual phone call is like most recent ones, talking about work and a bit about Nicole. But this time, he talks about his faith. "I'm searching for the truth. I struggle with some things in the Bible." We try our best to an-swer his questions, but we know that he needs to come to grips with his own doubts. His relationship with Christ needed to be his own journey, not ours. I again enlisted the prayers of my close friends and family members. On my knees daily, I plead with my Lord to draw our son closer to Him and fight the battle for Tim that may be raging within him.

POSTLUDE

eleven

CAN YOU HEAR ME?

I AM IN DEEP EMOTIONAL PAIN, OVER-whelming darkness, and extreme fatigue. I feel like I'm in a dank, bottomless well that I can't climb out of and there's no hope. How did this happen? Some days I want to sleep forever, not opening my eyes, not dealing with anything. Other days I work on my computer applications and don't sleep for...has it really been three days since I slept? Sometimes I'm not sure if it's daytime or evening. I don't care about eating. Ordering delivery pizza is just easier than going out in the world, where I might have to deal with reality. Food doesn't really appeal to me anyway.

Sometimes the dark places are more than I can handle. During those dark times, I hear voices that I can't erase from my brain. They are controlling voices that overpower me, even scare me. They say, "You're not enough. Nobody would know or even care if you were gone from this earth."

Ironically, it's during this time I receive a phone call from someone from my past. Answering the phone, I hear "Tim, it's Devon. Remember, we went to grade school together?" I have not heard from Devon for many, many years. Memories of that broken arm, the ridicule he gave me and the bullying he inflicted on me come painfully flooding back. "I'm calling," Devon continues, "to find out how you're doing and to ask a very important question."

I tell him a bit about work, and we chat briefly about his current interests. "The main reason for this call is to ask your forgiveness." I am stunned! In the years since we'd spoken, time had erased much of the harshness of what I went through. "I know I was cruel to you and gave you grief when we were growing up. For that, I am really sorry. If you could find it in your heart to forgive me, I would be thankful."

It takes me time to respond, but eventually I say, "Devon, of course I forgive you. We were boys. Life is different now. And we don't know if tomorrow or the next day is our last. I forgive you, Devon, and I hope your life is happy."

I can tell in his voice he is greatly relieved when he finally responds, "Tim, you're quite a man to offer that forgiveness. I am grateful to you."

I hold on to that conversation for many days. Funny how things can turn around in life. My heart had hurt for Devon way back in eighth grade. It now has compassion for him as he struggles to forgive himself.

Meanwhile, my cloud continues to overshadow reality. My perception seems to be narrowing. What I feel is taking over; what I intellectually know is in the background. No one would understand if I told them any of this. Too weird. To most people, I probably look pretty normal on the outside. But I am living two lives, which is increasingly difficult for me. Those voices tell me that I should be ashamed, that I'm unforgiven, and that there is no hope for someone like me. I can forgive a person who hurt me, like Devon. I cannot forgive myself.

Mom and Pops call sometimes. I just let voicemail take their messages. I usually don't call back. I can't talk to them during these horrendously dark days. When I do call, I talk about work or tell them cute things about Wanda the cat. I haven't told them about taking medication for my depression. (Did I remember to take it today?) But I do mention that I'm reclusive and I like it that way. I don't want to deal with reality or people.

Sometimes taking my depression medicine makes me feel numb, or maybe just blah. I don't feel the highs that really perk me up. I also don't feel the extreme lows, which I guess is a good thing. But being numb is no way to live either. I know I am sick, but I don't know the remedy. I just want this pain of existence to stop.

twelve

A Surprise

IN AUGUST 2013, TIM SURPRISED US WITH A
visit to Colorado. He was contemplating moving out
west, and we relished the thought of having him closer to
us. He spent an entire week in our home, enjoying dinners
with us and talking about a new application he was working on that might go global once it was perfected. He cel-
ebrated our 41st anniversary with us. The dinner we shared
at a local restaurant with Tim, Joy and her family was full
of warm remembrances. After dinner that night, we all

walked through Old Town in Fort Collins. Joy and Tim walked arm-in-arm, something that hadn't happened for a very long time. The old-time candy shop we all walked through delighted Tim with its shelves of gum, soda pop in glass bottles, jawbreakers, and ropes of licorice from out of the past. The air that evening blossomed with the fragrance of hope.

The storm clouds brewed up once more with the events of the following day. Before Tim's return flight to Atlanta, we suggested visiting Hearts and Horses, my therapeutic riding center. We would give Tim a chance to visit some of my favorite horses. He loved the idea, so out to the foothills of Loveland we went. On the way to the center, Tim seemed unusually quiet. Upon arrival, Denny took off ahead of us. Without warning, Tim began sobbing uncontrollably, sinking to his knees in the dirt. I hugged him, bringing him closer to me. "Oh, Tim, please, please talk to me about this!" I cried, my eyes filling with tears for him. "I can't forgive myself," he finally said. "I just can't forgive who I am." There were no words to console him; finally, after many moments of sobbing, he stood up. Pulling himself together, he resolved, "Let's go see those horses." I was shocked and didn't know what to do. He seemed calmer after hugging a few of the gentle equines. He lingered out by the pasture, watching the horses run and feast on the grasses in the fields. I watched him as he gazed at the foothills. There was no life in his eyes. He seemed distant and distracted. Where had his joy for life gone? Where was the perky, quirky jubilant Tim we knew?

Looking at his watch, he determined that we should leave Hearts and Horses and head for Denver International Airport. And so, that day we reluctantly said goodbye to our son.

The hurting child inside that grown young man was calling out for help. I felt powerless to reach into his heart and put salve on his wounds. The illness he was experiencing was progressing, and I couldn't push back the winds of that storm.

When March of the following year rolled around, Tim called to thank me for the letter I wrote. He explained that for a portion of some weeks, he had slept very little, eaten only when he thought he was actually hungry, and worked all night on many occasions. Fortunately, he could work from home, so his business commitments remained the same, maybe even better, since he worked constantly for a period of time. He stated that he was on a more even keel, but the dark days were hard to overcome. Previously, he had told us he was taking depression medication, and that it helped. "But Mom," he said, "feeling just blah is no picnic either." In fact, Tim said there were days he thought about ending it all. He relished the highs and preferred not to be numb, even though the lows eventually became horrible.

Both Denny and I worried. And prayed. And tried our best to stay in touch with our dear son, who seemed to be slipping away. He was a grown man with a life of his own, a successful, caring 36-year-old who tried with all his might to survive.

Tim's phone call put us into panic mode. Do we immediately fly out to Georgia and find help from a mental health professional? Do we intervene? Sit down with him and discuss his medication? Would he welcome Mom and Dad interfering with his personal life? How serious was this? Do we trust that his doctors were doing all that they could? Was he getting help besides medication?

thirteen

My Final Song

I WAS GLAD FOR THAT LAST VISIT TO MY Colorado home in August. I was able to meet with my cousins and some of my friends, spend quality time with my family, and laugh and hug each one of them. This was a time for reconciliation with those I loved, a time that was good for my soul. I stayed one week just soaking in their love, but also giving them good memories. Mom asked if I was thinking of moving from Georgia back to Colorado, since my lease on my apartment would be up after the first of next year. I discussed the cost of living in Colorado, which could make it prohibitive for me. But coming home sounded good to me.

Saying goodbye to Mom and Pops was one of the hardest things I have ever done. I couldn't explain to them what was going on in my head, so I just sobbed "I'm so sorry," and allowed Mom to hold and hug me for a short while. If they knew what this visit was really about and what would happen soon, it would have broken them. I left for Georgia that August afternoon knowing the end was approaching.

Upon arriving at my apartment, I made preparations for my final months. I continued to have questions such as, "Should I hang on for one more day? For what? Things won't get any better." My perception of my situation continued to be restricted, squeezing out any instinctual hope that I had.

I notified the apartment complex of my move so mail would be stopped at a certain date. I chose "exit" songs to listen to on my iPod as I took my final breaths. I bought enough food for Wanda and left it where Nicole could find it so she could continue to care for our baby cat. I met with some of my coworkers a few days before my "exit" to tie up any loose ends. Lunch with Nicole the day before went smoothly. All was in place, and I was at peace. I felt like I finally had control of my life, something I hadn't felt in a long, long time.

fourteen

THE DAY HIS MUSIC DIED

MOTHER'S DAY, MAY 11, 2014.
On this day, I love that God has gifted my life with children and a grandchild. Going to church with Joy, her husband, and our grandson brought me a sense of peace. After the service, we helped set up cots in classrooms and offices for the homeless to stay in during the week. Lunch was specially prepared at Joy's house by the three master chefs; our daughter, her husband, and her son. Their meals are always a treat. During lunch, my cell

phone rang. Picking it up, I expected to hear Tim's voice. It had been six weeks since we had last heard from him. Earlier that day, I had committed to calling him that evening if he didn't get in touch with us. However, he usually called on this special day.

"Hi, Mom." It was Nicole. She had an unusual tone in her voice, sort of shaky. "Have you heard from Tim today?" I told her no, but I was sure he would call. I promised to call her back if I heard anything. Tim and Nicole texted or called each other almost every day, so I became a bit worried. Back at the lunch table in Joy's kitchen, I relayed Nicole's message to them. Something in the back of my mind told me I should be concerned. But it was Mother's Day—he would call and everything would be okay. We played some family games, but as the minutes ticked on, I became increasingly anxious. "We better head for home and try to get in touch with Tim," I nudged Denny. Joy and her husband's faces reflected concern.

At home, Denny and I texted Tim and left voicemails on his cell phone. We waited. No response. We tried to have a bite of dinner, but neither of us wanted to eat. "I'll contact one of his co-workers to see if he has seen Tim recently," Denny offered. The call revealed that Tim had met several of the guys for lunch the previous Wednesday. They talked about the global launch of the new application they were working on. All had seemed positive. During Nicole's original call, she said that she and Tim had gone out for lunch just yesterday, and he seemed upbeat.

Still no response from Tim. The minutes seemed slow and drawn out. Time was standing still. There was a knock at the door. Denny answered it and I could hear a man's voice talking briefly. Denny invited him in, along with two women. I came around the corner of our entryway to see a uniformed sheriff's deputy and two victim advocates. I knew immediately what he was going to say.

"We have received word from Canton, Georgia, that your son, Tim, is deceased." My hands flew up to my face in shock and my knees buckled. My heart was in my throat. I felt as if I could barely breathe. "Do you know any details?" I finally choked out. Somehow Denny and I invited them to sit in our great room.

"The sheriff's office told us that he has taken his own life, and the time of death was this morning." They sat with us and gently gave us that sheriff's phone number so he could reveal other details. He gave Denny phone numbers and names to contact for making arrangements. The victim advocates kindly gave us brochures where we could find emotional help, including grief support groups, mental health resources, and therapists. All of those moments are still a blur to both of us. We were in deep shock.

Since I was unable to think, breathe, or control the shaking in my body, the victim advocates asked if there were any people they could notify for us. Our first response was, "Our daughter, but we will call her ourselves." Denny somehow got enough inner strength to pick up the phone. I could hear his voice struggling as he spoke extremely difficult words to Joy: "Tim has died." Through the receiver I could hear her painful scream, "No, no, it can't be...it's Mother's Day!!!" Her screams continued until her husband took the phone and told Denny they would get in the car and be over to our house shortly.

Upon the arrival of Joy, her husband, and their 11-year-old son, we embraced each other, sobbing, as we shared the searing pain in our hearts. We had, for the most part, been a very close family. To have an essential member of that unit yanked from our midst, stripping the bonds that held us close, was totally unthinkable and tragic. Not being able to say goodbye to him was earth-shattering. To know that he would never, ever come walking through our door again and that we'd never hear his deep bass voice on the other end of the phone was unfathomable.

We felt our hearts being ripped apart, like the major portion of them died right along with Tim. At first, we couldn't believe such a thing could ever happen. We were in a fog, an unreal place that none of us had ever encountered.

Once we could compose ourselves for a moment, we called Nicole. She tearfully related that she had let the sheriff into Tim's apartment when he hadn't responded to her text messages. Upon entering the apartment, the sheriff noticed extra cans of cat food on top of Wanda's carrier. Tim cared enough to make sure Wanda was taken care of.

Deputies searched for his car and found Tim in it at a nearby park. He had taken his life in a very gentle way. Inside his car was my note to him about my hopes of having him move home someday. He moved to his heavenly home that Mother's Day, May 11, 2014, his birthday into eternal life.

But we, his loving family, were left here on Earth in the aftermath of the most horrendous storm any of us had encountered in our lives. "How can we go on living without this vital member of our family? Will our hearts ever begin to heal and not feel the searing pain of our loss? Will life ever seem 'normal' again? Where is hope in the middle of this despair?" The music was gone.

fifteen

REBIRTH OF THE SONG

*P*ART OF THE PROCESS (OF REBIRTH) IS THE
*growth of a new relationship with the dead that "veri-
table ami mort" Saint-Exupery speaks of. Like all gestation, it
is a slow, dark, wordless process. While it is taking place, one is
painfully vulnerable. One must guard and protect the new life
growing within—like a child.*

—Anne Morrow Lindberg

Grief is not lack of faith or weakness,
but it is the price of love.
—Anonymous

How does one go on living, breathing, existing once a treasured loved one has left the earth? Where is the hope? What do we cling to when all supports seem gone? Those were our questions in the moments after Tim died.

The day after hearing the news, close friends arrived at our house to hug us, pray with us, and comfort us with specially-prepared food, handknit shawls, and other tokens of their love. Joy had spent the night with us so that we wouldn't be alone. The following morning, Joy came into our bedroom. I welcomed her to lie beside us as she had done on mornings when she was much younger. We lay beside each other, wondering if we had just experienced a horrible nightmare, hoping we would wake up. But it was all painfully real, and we just held each other and sobbed with heart-wrenching cries. We were unsure if our next breaths would come into our lungs, and our chests ached like our hearts had been stabbed into millions of pieces.

Later that morning, Joy's dear friend from high school, Valerie, came up to Fort Collins from Denver to console her and to make a meal for us. In the afternoon,

I laid down in our bedroom to try to take a nap. I drifted in and out of sleep until I was suddenly awakened by an ear-shattering scream. Thinking our grandson might have fallen, I ran out to the great room to see Valerie crying uncontrollably. Joy was holding her. "What happened?" I asked.

Valerie couldn't get any words out in the middle of her sobs. But Joy told me Valerie had gotten a call from her mother; Valerie's brother-in-law had died in a traffic accident. He was younger than Tim and left behind two young daughters and his loving wife, Valerie's sister.

After all of us caught our breath enough to speak, we all questioned, "How can this be?" Two tragedies of young men losing their lives over the course of two days. Although it was mid-afternoon with the sun shining outside, the storm clouds within our home hung dark and threatening over all of us. There seemed to be no light, no end to the torrential rains within our hearts. We just held each other until no more tears were left to shed. No one ate any of the special food Valerie had prepared or friends had brought over for us.

Denny spoke lovingly later that evening. "We need to make preparations to drive to Georgia to take care of Tim's affairs and be with Nicole." Joy's husband, our action man in the family, made calls to rent an SUV that could hold his family, Denny and me, and extra room to bring back some of Tim's possessions. We decided to leave the next morning. Valerie spent the night at Joy's home. In the morning, we all drove to Denver to console Valerie's sister and family before heading south to Georgia.

We journeyed to Nashville on our way to Tim's apartment in Canton. Joy's husband's sister had graciously invited our grandson to stay with her family so that he could be with cousins as we took care of things down south.

Driving to Georgia was a trip we hadn't willingly chosen for the purpose we had to face. Every mile along the way meant one of us sobbing or reflecting on the last hours we had endured together. But we were TOGETHER. We talked, prayed, and even began the dreaded task of thinking about the funeral. Joy used her cell phone to research and call funeral homes in the Canton area. She called our church in Fort Collins to begin putting together the details of the memorial service.

We arrived in Canton, Georgia, after two very long days on the road. The rain along the way did not make it any easier. It symbolized what was going on in our souls. Nicole greeted us at her apartment along with a co-worker of Tim's, and together we went to Tim's place. Entering that empty home of his—the place he listened to his music, played his electronic piano, worked on his computer, shared time with Wanda the cat, spent years with Nicole, and called home—was next to impossible without sobs of grief and deep, deep sadness. We expected to see him pop out of the closet and shout, "Just fooling," and wished that he actually would.

Going through his things and placing them in boxes as if we were bringing him home from college again felt so shallow. An entire life filled with memories and emotions was relegated to cardboard containers. He was known to wear T-shirts most days, so Nicole went through all his T-shirts and laundered them so she could keep them as a remembrance of his physical presence.

Tim's co-worker Nathan generously proposed having a celebration of Tim's life at a local restaurant so that many of his friends could attend. He arranged all the details and notified Tim's acquaintances of the event. We were pleasantly surprised by the outpouring of love and respect that was shown at this get-together. People from all over the US attended. In addition, Nathan arranged to have Google Hangout on his laptop during the evening so those who couldn't make it in person would be a part of the event. We knew that Tim was highly respected in his field and his knowledge of Lotus Notes was vast, but we had no idea what people's interactions with him had been. Each person, whether in the States, Germany, Belgium, the Netherlands, or the UK, told us that it was Tim's kind heart that they would always remember. No matter how busy Tim was or what he was involved with, he would drop everything to help them. If they had a computer difficulty, even if it was a simple matter, Tim was willing to show them how to navigate it. That is what bolstered us the most during the difficult first days—knowing he was remembered for the things that mattered, like helping others out of the kindness of his heart. The T-shirts Nicole had laundered were placed over the backs of each chair in the restaurant event room, making it seem as if Tim were there celebrating with us. Some of his friends even donned one of Tim's shirts over their own in remembrance of him. We were overwhelmingly touched by this outpouring of love from his friends!

The healing began as we drove back to Fort Collins with a few boxes of his belongings: cherished books (he collected hundreds); CDs (again, too many to take all of them); photo albums; yearbooks; awards; clippings of his haircut when his curls were long; his grandfather's music box; sheet music; posters from the many drama productions he was involved with; barbershop chorus memories and other bits and pieces of the life of our only son.

The memorial service in Fort Collins brought over 400 individuals, including friends from high school, college, and people from far and wide who had known him as a youngster or had contact with him as an adult. More healing occurred during this service, but we were still numb. It just didn't sink in that this vibrant, talented, quirky guy would not be coming home again.

That kind of healing only comes after time. Someone told us we will get through this, but we will never get over this. Each of us started the grieving process in our own unique way.

We felt very fortunate to have so many resources in our community to assist us through the wilderness of grief. The local chapter of the Alliance for Suicide Prevention held group support meetings, where we met others going through similar situations. The meetings provided helpful suggestions to bring about some healing. Through these meetings, it became evident we were not alone, and the feelings we were having were normal. Repeatedly, we heard that one person grieves differently from another and there is no right or wrong way to grieve. Another thing that gave us comfort was learning that the healing process may be wave-like. Sometimes we'd feel like we were finally on top of things, and then we'd hit a low point again. How true! Knowing this ahead of time helped us to cope when it happened, to know we weren't just going crazy! The Alliance also had a lending library of helpful books, including *Dying to Be Free* by Beverly Cobain and Jean Larch and *Understanding Your Suicide Grief* by Alan D. Wolfelt. Resources like these were valuable when we felt so alone in our grief.

Crazy: that's how we felt for a good part of the first

few months after Tim died. We couldn't put our thoughts together in any organized fashion. We would forget simple things or dates, and trying to find where we last put our reading glasses was impossible some days. It was very true what some had told us: Don't make any important decisions the first year after a loved one dies. I know why!

Our daughter and family were fortunate enough to have a counselor who allowed them to talk out their feelings of anger, abandonment, sadness, and fear. She offered suggestions to move them forward, such as writing down 100 ways to be good to yourself. Pulling that list out when a person is having a challenging day can bring relief. Writing down memories of the loved one is also cathartic and can also bring about laughter, which seems impossible in the first months after a loss.

All the steps we took immediately after Tim's departure brought about a bit of restoration. However, the defining moments of healing involved intimacy with my Lord. At the moment when the sheriff delivered the news on that Mother's Day, I pleaded with God, "Be near!" And instantly He was. He pulled me to His chest and held me there until I felt His breath become my own when I was unable to breathe. He whispered in my ear His Word, "My grace is sufficient for you, for my power is made perfect in weakness." (2 Corinthians 12:9)

In the months that followed, I had many questions,

as did most of our family. I called his doctor and asked questions such as, "Did Tim receive recent news of other health issues that would have caused him to take his own life?"

"He was on medicine for depression, which was the only thing he was seen for," she shared with me. So the question was, did he stop taking his medication? In a recent phone call, he had mentioned he didn't like the numbing effect it caused, stating he had no highs or lows.

Our family also began the "what-ifs" that come with guilt. "If only I had been there more for him when he tried to withdraw, maybe he would have reached out to me." "What if I had tried to get some help for him, or just listened to him to try to understand the pain he was going through?" These are common questions of many who have lost a loved one to suicide. But it's important to remember that depression, bipolar disorder, and any mental illness are complicated diseases that can lead to a person wanting to be done with the associated pain. Instead of looking back at the way Tim died, we began focusing on how he lived. We wanted to continue the kindness and compassion he exhibited while he was alive.

We look at life differently now. We treasure the small moments: the glitter of new-fallen snow in the sunlight, the hue of autumn leaves, the sound of birds on a summer day. Our family members and friends are even more precious to us now. The story of Christ's coming to Earth on that first Christmas has more of an impact, knowing He gave up His heavenly position to be humbled, to be born among us. God gave His only Son to save my only son for eternity. What a sacrifice!

Now, several months after Mother's Day, looking back on Tim's birth 36-plus years ago, we are thankful he has a new birth into eternity. He is a new creature. He is pain-free. He can soar like wings of eagles. His spirit is flying without the chains that bound him to this sin-filled world. I think about a bird, created to fly, that is caged. After many years of imprisonment, the door is opened. He flies out into the open, feeling the wind through his feathers, seeing everything he's missed from the heights. The freedom he feels fills his soul with a joy he's never experienced. This little bird is our son now. To fly hand-in-hand with the Holy Spirit in freedom must be exhilarating. I would want nothing less for my child.

HOPE

"Hope" is the thing with feathers
that perches in the soul—
And sings the tune without the words—
And never stops—at all—
—Emily Dickinson

sixteen

SONG OF HOPE AND HELP

YES, I AM FREE OF EARTHLY BOUNDS, BUT I feel the urgent need to speak to my family, my friends, and the community about suicide and mental illness. A number of things need to change so others like me can be helped.

1. Recognize the problem. Don't be afraid to question your friends and family members to see how they're doing.

2. Society must perceive mental health issues differently. If someone broke an arm, friends would rush to sign the cast. If someone has a mental health issue, friends tend to run away. The brain is just another portion of the human body.

3. If someone has clinical depression, it's not just a matter of being sad over something that happened. Feeling sad about the loss of a loved one or the breakup of a relationship is normal. Being depressed when things are going great? That could be depression. It's an illness, not a choice. Thinking happy thoughts won't cure this illness. And making the choice to get over it is not an option.

4. If a friend or family member who may have depression doesn't call or contact you as often as you'd like, don't take it personally, be hurt by it, or get angry! Check in with that person, because a hallmark of severe depression is an inability to do anything. I would have done anything to feel good enough to call the ones I loved.

5. Teach acceptance of ourselves. We all hurt. We all need to heal.

6. If you have a mental illness, realize you are sick, not weak. Reach out for help.

7. No one is perfect. Take away the taboos of mental illness.

8. Learn to love ourselves. Stand strong with others who can support you.
9. Stop saying someone "committed" suicide. A criminal "commits" a crime like murder or robbery. Suicide is a public health issue, not a crime. Saying the loved one took his or her own life may be gentler on the survivors.
10. Make treatment more available. Create shorter wait times for patients to be seen by professionals.
11. Stop the silence. Families, talk to one another. Friends, support each other. Teachers, take time each day to connect with students. Medical personnel, take the time to evaluate the health of your patient's WHOLE body, including their emotions.
12. Listen to and accept each other without judgement or trying to fix the other person.

To my family, I would like to say hug each other a little tighter, enjoy each moment that has been given to you, remember that golden memories will always be yours, and live with purpose and passion so the world knows why you've been given one more day! Remember how I lived, not died, and then glimpse forever, for that's where I am.
—"Timmer"

seventeen

HOPE FOR "STORM SURVIVORS"

FIRST OF ALL, HOPE SEEMED AS FAR AWAY as the most distant planet when our precious son died. We felt alone, shocked, in deep anguish, anger, guilt, and a tiny bit of relief that he didn't have to suffer with the depression any longer. But hope? Oh my, no! Especially when we were unsure where our next breath would come from or when the next heartbeat within our weary chests would happen. We also felt very, very isolated. Everyone else continued on with life, laughing, going about their daily duties and going to bed at night to sleep. We couldn't imagine sleeping through the night, and if we did catch a few moments of rest, we'd wake up hoping this was all just a nightmare.

When we were in Georgia packing up Tim's belongings, we went to a restaurant to try to eat, even though food seemed so unappetizing. Joy remarked on the people sitting around tables, laughing and carrying on like nothing had happened. But our world had just stopped turning; tragedy jolted us to the very core, and no one else seemed to care. When the waitress came to take our order, no one at our table could utter a word without tears streaming down our faces. We felt so sorry for that poor gal. She had no idea what our problem was! We now get a bit of a chuckle from that story, wondering what she thought about our grieving faces!

We experienced many stages of grief: shock, sorrow, struggle, surrender, and, much farther down the road, sanctification and service. We all experienced these in different orders; we'd thought we made it through one stage, then go through it again. We'd feel a bit more able to take the next step, then we'd be hit once again. Up and down and backward, we felt as if we were on a rickety roller coaster, begging to get off.

But with the help of our angels—our understanding, patient friends and family members who carried us many days when we were so very weak—we made it through one more day. We received hundreds of cards, emails, Facebook messages, calls and letters. I wanted to thank each person who lovingly cared for us during those early days with a personal note, but with my hands spastic from multiple sclerosis, I couldn't address all those envelopes. My "Bookies" book club came to my rescue. Members arrived at our home with eager faces, hugs, pens, and hands willing to address numerous thank-you notes. After the task was completed, they stayed and listened to how my hurting heart was doing that day. Because of their compassion, healing began.

Hope in the midst of our storms in life allows for recovery, restoration, rebuilding, rebirth, and reconstruction. Rainbows cannot occur without the rain, and light must be present through the storm. God is that light, that hope that shines for us. At the very center of that hope is our Comforter, our Counselor, our Creator, and our Savior. He is the mighty fortress that we cling to and where we find security.

As we face each storm in life, our initial response may be fear. It certainly has been my initial response many times. The Bible has over 95 references to the gripping fear that most of us experience. But God always responds to the fear we feel with words of stillness for our souls: Isaiah 41:10, "So do not fear. I am with you."

When the entire world around us changes, He never wavers. And He looks in our eyes with compassion and invites us, "Come to me, all you who are weary and burdened, and I will give you rest." (Matthew 11:28). In James 5:11 we are told, "The Lord is full of compassion and mercy."

As I continue to heal and dry off from each rainstorm in my life, I sometimes feel battered and pummeled by the hail. Those hailstones were in the form of my struggles and diagnosis of MS, my husband's stroke on Father's Day a year after Tim's death, and my own heart surgery right before Denny's stroke.

There are times when I feel bloodied and wounded, as if I've been through a war in which I'm not sure who has won the battle. Deep down I know Who has won, but my finite brain and emotions take over as I sob from my losses. I feel like the illustration once given by a local artist about the potter and the clay. As the potter works with the clay to form a vessel, he will take the clay in his hand and literally slam it down on the work surface to force bubbles out. He may do that several times. The purpose? If he ignored that step, the vessel would likely crack when placed in the fire to harden. My storms have felt like that painful process. My Potter is forming me for the purpose He created me to fulfill. In that process, it's necessary to endure certain steps, but the Potter is right there through it all, even though the fire may bring about a transformation!

FIVE IMPORTANT LESSONS I'VE LEARNED FROM THE STORMS IN MY LIFE

1. These are not forever storms.

    The apostle Paul wrote in 2 Corinthians 4:17-18:

    "Therefore we do not lose heart. Though outwardly we are wasting away, yet inwardly we are being renewed day by day. For our light and momentary troubles are achieving for us an eternal glory that far outweighs them all. So we fix our eyes not on what is seen, but on what is unseen. For what is seen is temporary, but what is unseen is eternal."

    The pain of loss, the hardship of dreams dashed away, and the agony of having to spend one more day sifting through the rubble of tragedy sometimes clouds my long-distance vision. Even though I feel that there may be no way out of the muck, the Lord promises in His Word that this is only temporary, and eternity awaits. Focusing my faith-eyes on the eternal reward helps me to see beyond current challenges.

The story of a young athlete at a local track meet touched my heart. Running with all his might, he came to the first hurdle. He straddled it the best he could, but fell onto the hard pavement of the track. Picking himself up, he raced on. The next hurdle loomed in front of him, and determined, he jumped it, but again fell to the hard surface. Now bloodied, he once again persevered. By now the crowd saw he was last in the race and hoped he could make the next hurdle. With determination on his face, he pushed his body toward the third hurdle. Stretching his bleeding legs, lifting high, he pushed forward over it. His toe caught the hurdle; the crowd let out an agonized gasp and watched him fall once again. They were sure he'd walk over to the sidelines and give up. But he resolutely picked himself up one more time and continued the race. One last hurdle and he would be home free and at the finish line. Hobbling along on wounded legs, he mustered up all his strength and tried with all his might to clear the fourth and final hurdle. Success! He flew over the last obstacle! With his eyes fixed on the finish line and his teammates cheering him on, he ran into their arms, finishing the race with victory shining on his face. What did this young man's story teach me? He kept his eyes on the goal. He could have given up hope as injuries wracked his body with pain. But he never took his eyes off the finish line.

2. Circumstances may change, people may let me down, but God is always the same.

In Hebrews 13:8 we read, "Jesus Christ is the same yesterday and today and forever." Just when I think everything is going okay, life is pretty stable, the storms hit. When I'm sure a wonderful friend will be there for me when I'm having a bad day, her support may not be available. That is because she is human, and the storms in this sinful world will always be brewing. But God is solid, firmer than the huge boulders of the Rocky Mountains. One of my favorite Lutheran hymns gives me comfort: "My Hope is Built on Nothing Less" by Edward Mote. Written in 1834, it is based on 1 Timothy 1:1.

My hope is built on nothing less
Than Jesus' blood and righteousness;
I dare not trust the sweetest frame,
But wholly lean on Jesus' name.

On Christ, the solid Rock, I stand;
All other ground is sinking sand.
When darkness veils His lovely face,
I rest on His unchanging grace;
In every high and stormy gale
My anchor holds within the veil.
On Christ, the solid Rock, I stand;
All other ground is sinking sand.

His oath, His covenant, and blood
Support me in the whelming flood;
When ev'ry earthly prop gives way,
He then is all my Hope and Stay.
On Christ, the solid Rock, I stand;
All other ground is sinking sand.

3. There are treasures in the rubble.

After the June 2012 High Park forest fire in Colorado, rescue workers sifted through the ashen ruins. I watched those workers at a home behind my brother's mountain house in Glacier View. This home had burnt to the ground; only the foundation remained. I witnessed hours of grueling labor in an effort to find something of value in the rubble. But after all that work, a volunteer would hold up a photo which was spared from the scorching flames or a piece of jewelry that meant so much to its owner. A treasure! Through my personal challenges, those types of treasures have emerged: a more compassionate heart for others who have their own challenges; a capacity to listen fully when someone tells their story; and a trust in my Lord, who is in control and I am not! I now value, more than ever, the people God has placed in my life, including precious family members, friends I love dearly, even strangers I meet on a daily basis. I look at the world with different eyes now: the delicate beauty of the first crocus blooming in the spring; the lilting sound of the red-winged blackbirds on the lake behind our house; the laughter of a little child; the smell of fresh-baked bread; the look of love in the eyes of a very dear friend. These are small treasures, but they are also gifts from God that help me hold my head above water and hold onto hope.

4. I can choose to be bitter or better.

In Sarah Young's devotional book, *Jesus Calling*, she writes about Jesus' words to us based upon Ephesians 3: 20-21; Romans 8:6;

Isaiah 40:30-31; and Revelation 5:13:

"I am able to do far beyond all that you ask or imagine. Come to Me with positive expectations, knowing that there is no limit to what I can accomplish. Ask My Spirit to control your mind, so that you can think great thoughts of Me. Do not be discouraged by the fact that many of your prayers are yet unanswered. Time is a trainer, teaching you to wait upon Me, to trust Me in the dark. The more extreme your circumstances, the more likely you are to see MY POWER AND GLORY at work in the situation. Instead of letting difficulties draw you into worrying, try to view them as setting the scene for My glorious intervention. Keep your eyes and your mind wide open to all that I am doing in your life."

5. The energy that consumed my grieving for what was lost can be turned to a positive action, fulfilling His purpose for my life.

When Tim died, at first my cup of grief was overflowing with bitter tears, extreme heartache, and pain-filled sorrow. "What can I do with all this anguish?" I pleaded with God. His answer seemed to be, "Turn it into good with My help."

In the days, weeks, and months of the first year after losing my son, I realized I was still a mother, but now in a new way. I was still a mother to my daughter and a grandmother to my grandson. I was a wife, a friend, a leader of Bible studies, and a communicator to others who were going through losses.

A new ministry emerged when I grabbed the opportunity to begin a local chapter of the Lutheran Church Charities' K-9 Comfort Dog Ministry at our church. Through this compassionate outreach to members of our church and the community, I was given the chance to listen to others' stories of loss. Because of my own losses, I was able to listen with new ears and bring some comfort to hurting individuals. God used negatives and storms in my life to bring about positives for His will to be done. I just had to be open to those nudges in my life from the Holy Spirit, and let Him lead me to new vistas.

Ann Voskamp writes, "Our storms can be canvases for God's lightning glory." I wait with expectant HOPE as God paints his masterpiece through all these storms!

eighteen

Voices of Hope from Joshua and AJ

IN RECENT DAYS, OUR COMMUNITY HAS been touched over and over again by the suicides of precious sons and daughters. Cubby the K-9 Comfort Dog and I have visited high schools that are reeling from the loss of their students, and together we weep. Young lives, so vibrant, so full of potential, have been cut short.

Two of those students, if here today, would speak out with important messages, just like our son Tim. Their mothers have vital words to share with you about what it's

like to survive the death of their precious children. But most importantly, they share the hope that has sustained them through the moments, days, and months.

Joshua's Story

Part One: Joshua's Story

My name is Robin, and I am a 45-year-old single mother of three children, ages 25, 15, and 14. I have three kids, yet there is a huge hole in my heart because one is gone.

My 15-year-old son, Joshua, shot himself in the head on November third, 2016, at his high school. He instantly died.

Joshua was very smart and even the detectives could not believe the electronic and technical expertise he had. He wanted to be an electrical engineer. He and I were very close.

Even though Joshua is no longer here on Earth, we have amazing memories and I would like to share a few fun stories of our mischief!

One day, his brother Caleb and I toilet-papered the inside of our house. We thought it would be funny to see Joshua's reaction when he came home. I think we used about 20 rolls of toilet paper. He looked so perplexed and the look on his face was really worth all the clean-up!

At the middle school and high school he attended, there are ceiling tiles——the ones that are white with holes in them. Joshua would daily find pencils and throw them into these ceiling tiles. He wanted to get really good at it, so we literally bought some of these and nailed them to his ceiling of his room so he could practice! He could make them stick in one try! One student said that the day they were able to go back to school after the suicide, many students threw pencils into the ceiling in honor of Josh. The teachers let them stay there for a while. But I do feel bad for contributing to this——I bet the custodians were not too happy!

We would drive around town and Joshua would yell, "I LOVE YOU!" to random people like joggers or construction workers. It was ALWAYS hilarious to see their reactions. We laughed A LOT.

So…back to Joshua's suicide…I did not see any signs at all. It was a total surprise and we had had such a great night the night before. He ate a whole pumpkin pie and the last words I said to him were, "Goodnight, I love you."

His dad was on a business trip in London at the time, and I was pet-sitting his dog for him. I get up early for work, and when I took his dog outside, I noticed my garage was open and my car was missing. My first thought was that someone stole my car—that could be replaced. But I immediately wanted to check on my two boys! I ran to Joshua's room first and his bed was empty. My heart was pounding as I ran downstairs to check on Caleb and he was sound asleep.

Thankfully, I have always been able to handle emergency situations pretty well. The impact always hits me later. I called his dad in London and he did not answer. I chose to call 911. I told them that my son and my car were missing and I did not know where they were. I was still in the mindset that someone had come into the house and taken him and stolen my car.

The 911 operator asked me if I had any idea where he may be. The first place I thought of was his dad's house, which is only about five miles away. The second place I thought of was the high school. They sent officers to both places to check. So I had to wait.

Many people have asked me why I thought of the high school afterward. I thought of it because if Joshua could get to school at 5 a.m., he would. He always wanted to stay after school…I think he just liked being there.

With fear in my heart, I went downstairs to wake up Caleb. I asked him if he knew where his brother could be. As soon as he was coherent enough, he got a worried look in his eyes and said, "I don't know, but Joshua came down here late last night and asked me how late the custodians work at the school. I told him I have no idea." Then we waited.

While we waited we were thinking of all the trouble he was going to be in and discussed this laughing (maybe as a coping strategy?). We talked about how he was only 15 and stole a car and if he was at the high school it was probably not for a good reason. He had been getting into trouble recently, so we were thinking he was just doing something stupid and was going to be in a lot of trouble with the law.

When I finally got ahold of his dad, I was calm and just told him Joshua and my car were missing and the police were going to check his house and the school. My ex-husband, being a county sheriff, instantly called other deputies for help. He called me back and said, "I know your mind has gone there." I asked him, "No...where?!" He replied, "If he is found we have to be prepared that it is not going to be good." I still did not understand, but when it hit me I fell to the floor crying. Poor Caleb had no idea what his dad had said, so we hung up and I told him we needed to be prepared. Then we were just frightened and turned on the news to see if we could learn anything, anything at all.

Suddenly, Caleb let out the most painful sound I have ever heard in my life. He found out on social media that his brother had taken his life at the high school. That is how we found out. It was horrific.

About five minutes later, the police arrived to tell us what we already knew. Within a very short amount of time, several officers came, and they called Joshua's dad in London to tell him that his son had died and that it looked like a self-inflicted gunshot wound.

The rest of that day is a blur. I remember being really concerned for Caleb, but was held up by different officers and detectives. The forensic police van arrived. Curious neighbors came over. The detectives asked for my written permission to go through our house to search for anything. They were, and rightly so, concerned about it being at the school and wanted to see if there were any clues to his motive. My daughter and son-in-law came over, and this helped tremendously, as I was completely overwhelmed. I was so worried about Caleb, I was getting angry with all the questions, but there was not anything I could do it seemed. I really needed his dad. I kept thinking that if he were there, it would be a million times easier, because he is a sheriff with a very level head, and extremely logical.

Because Joshua's dad contacted other deputies, thankfully they were the ones who found Joshua's body and not a student or teacher. This was at the exact same time that all the kids were arriving to start school. Obviously, they shut the school down and sent them home. Many students' parents complained about the timing of being told, but the sheriffs literally found his body at the same time school was about to start.

The detectives were searching my house for any explosives, weapons, any kind of evidence that he may have had intentions of hurting anyone else. I gave them permission to take anything they needed. One made a comment on how brilliant he must have been with technology and electronics due to things he found in his room.

The school district and sheriff office closed the school for two days, searching for anything that may harm other students. As a mom, it was so awful to think that my son would hurt anyone else. Yet…he did hurt himself…fatally. I felt like I did not know my son at all.

My daughter and son-in-law drove Caleb and me to a place where they interview minors. Caleb was willing to answer any questions. The detectives took me in first and asked me the best way to approach Caleb. I remember telling them that he is very mature and would probably prefer direct questions, rather than ambiguous questions to get him to answer. He seemed to be gone a long time, but came out and said it went fine and he answered all of their questions.

Then, because it was not as chaotic with people all around us, reality set in. Joshua was gone. He killed himself. Why?? I think we will be asking ourselves that question the rest of our days here on earth.

Suddenly it seemed as if our whole small town wanted to help. I get overwhelmed easily, and this was extreme. I do not really remember the first couple of days, other than I started to tell people to stop hugging me, I just couldn't stand one more hug. I was all hugged out. And of course every time someone came over, it took me away from Caleb, my daughter, and son-in-law to be together and process.

As I look back I am so grateful for the people who came over instantly. It would frustrate me when people would just show up and not call or text to be sure I was able to even see anyone, as overwhelmed as I was. However, the community immediately started a meal plan for us, a funding page online, and brought practical supplies, gifts, flowers, money, offered assistance. I cannot remember how I was recommended to do this, but I started a list of random things I truly needed. When people would ask me, "How can we help?" or say, "Is there anything we can do for you?" I did not even know how to get my next breath, let alone anything else. Having a list was awesome. People appreciated helping in practical ways. Some of my ideas were so odd, but the loving community came through with EVERYTHING! Some things I had written down were thank-you cards, stamps, kitty litter, toilet paper, and to call someone I should call and let them know I will not be attending an appointment or activity I had committed to before this. I even left my printer on the front porch with a note, asking if someone really wanted to help, to help me fix it, because it had been broken for months. A couple days later, someone brought over a new printer that was a thousand times better than my broken one! Someone else brought over a brand-new freezer for all the food we would be receiving. I started a list and posted it on the door. I began to put notes on my door to let people know if it was a good or bad time for a visit. If we were in an intense conversation or just needed some quiet, it really helped. It also helped to put a note on the door that sometimes read "We NEED visitors!! Please ring the doorbell!" because it was like a pendulum—back and forth between needing people and needing quiet.

I wish I could list all of the names, non-profits, and organizations that helped in those first few weeks. I was in such a fog, honestly, that some I do not remember, and we received so many cards and gifts it was hard to keep up. My mom and dad came up from Arizona to help, which helped a lot, especially when I would get overwhelmed.

Part Two: How I handled it

It seemed as though suddenly everyone was gone and I was alone. Caleb's dad was back from London (he took three different planes to get home as fast as he possibly could), and Caleb is very close with his dad and wanted to be there, especially with his younger brother and sister to be there for them. I totally understood his need to be there. Yet there I was. No more revolving doors of guests, my parents went home, my daughter and son-in-law went back home, Caleb was at his dad's, and there I was in the quiet house...alone. Isolation can be a dark place sometimes.

Grieving as a single mom is a whole different animal than a married couple. Nights were the worst. Because I was grieving, I started isolating myself and pushing everyone away. I began to drink more and more to numb the pain.

We were going to spread Joshua's ashes on his birthday, November 27th. I honestly did not want to see my baby like that, basically burned to ashes. I want to remember him as I last saw him—laughing, saying he loved me. So the night before, I drank a lot of liquor and was so inebriated that I thought, "I could be with Joshua if I just take a bunch of pills." Of course, had I been sober, I never would have thought that, but tempting with alcohol is something the adversary uses to entice people to do things they normally would not do.

Joshua's dad had not heard from me, and since he has a key to my house he came to check on me. I was still alive and very angry that he found me. He called 911 and suddenly there were what seemed like 10 people in my bedroom all talking at the same time. I went by ambulance to the emergency room. I then spent nine days at a mental health hospital. Actually, I learned a lot of good coping strategies there. But then I got out and went back home and was alone at night once again. I did great for about a week and then started drinking again, because my grief was just too much to bear.

We had postponed the trip to spread Joshua's ashes to New Year's Eve instead, since I kind of crashed the first trip. Well, after drinking again and knowing I did not want to see my baby like that, I thought I could get out of going if I said I wanted to hurt myself. So, back to the mental health hospital again, this time for five days. The family went without me to spread his ashes. I still do not think they understand why I could not see Joshua like that. I just can't.

I went to an intensive outpatient therapy program for two weeks and went to Alcoholics Anonymous. Things started to look up and my entire day was not filled with sorrow over losing Joshua and over being alone. I was sober for 40 days and felt great, looked great, could handle things better…

Everyone says, "Grief comes in waves." Well, a tidal wave of anxiety, depression, PTSD, loneliness, grief, and despair washed over me. Once again, I went to alcohol. This time, though, I got really sick. I am so glad! I went to the doctor and checked myself into rehab this time. Seven days later I came out and it's only been a couple weeks at the time of this writing. I'm doing well. I go to at least one Alcoholics Anonymous meeting every day.

Some other feelings I felt were a sense of not knowing who I was anymore, like I was in another dimension, like it did not really happen. Oh how I wanted that to be true so badly! Each day seems to be different with emotions.

I share my story because if another mom (especially a single mom) has feelings like me, I am hoping to help her feel that it is not unusual.

Part Three: My Hope

I have always been a positive person. However, losing one of my children, who was only 15 years old, totally changed my life. It is deeper now, which is a strange word to use. I'm still positive, but mostly when I am around other people and busy. It's genuine, as well, not a false pretense. My grief comes when I am alone.

I have been a believer for almost 20 years. After Joshua died, I was extremely angry at God. If He knows how many hairs are on our heads...if He knows us even before we were in the womb...then He knew this was going to happen. Why? Why did it have to be me to lose a child to suicide? Why would He want me to suffer the deepest, most heart-wrenching pain ever?

I made a rash decision that I was not going to be a Christian any longer. I would be Buddhist, or New Age, or something else. But it was only a short matter of time before the Lord lured me back and I was running to His arms.

In this life, we *will* suffer loss and pain. This is a promise Paul stated in 1 Peter 1: 6-8: "In this you greatly rejoice, though now for a little while you may have had to *suffer grief* in all kinds of trials. These have come so that your faith—of greater worth than gold, which perishes even though refined by fire—may be proved genuine and may result in praise, glory and honor when Jesus Christ is revealed."

It is still very early in my grieving to say I have all hope. However, I find that helping others and not thinking about myself all the time REALLY helps. I am beginning to speak to different church groups locally telling Joshua's story and helping other single moms of teenagers in particular.

One thing I hear is, "everything happens for a reason." This is the most ridiculous cliché ever. Everything does not happen for a reason. God did not want our children to commit suicide, but this is another sign of our free will. Grief, pain, and suffering came into this world through Adam and Eve. Because of their disobedience, God promised there would be pain and sorrow because of their sin. Do I think that God can use us moms to help other moms? Absolutely! But I still believe, with all my heart, that God did not want Joshua to take his own life. Same with your child's life.

Talking about Joshua helps me heal. Especially when I tell others a funny story about him. We had so much fun together and I think it is important for him to be remembered for who he was his entire life, not just the one day that he decided to end it.

Joshua's dad, on the other hand, finds his strength in helping one-on-one with other teens. Talking about Joshua helps him as well, but not in public to groups like it does for me. It was extremely important for me to realize that everybody grieves differently. Once I accepted this, it helped me not seem as crazy.

Today I have a hope in seeing him again one day, on the other side. I believe whole-heartedly in Jesus Christ, the Holy Spirit, and the Father. I pray every night for God to hug him for me. It is just something I do that gives me comfort. Do I think that really happens? I don't know, but I find comfort in trusting God with my son now.

Regarding spiritual reality, I would like to share some verses that have spoken to me the most during this grieving period that has been so short, since Josh took his life only a few months ago.

In John 10:10, Jesus says, "The thief comes only to kill and destroy; I came that they may have life, and have it abundantly."

Romans 8:38-39—and I love The Message translation on this one where Paul says—"I'm absolutely convinced that nothing - **nothing** living or dead, angelic or demonic, today or tomorrow, high or low, thinkable or unthinkable - absolutely **nothing** can get between us and God's love because of the way that Jesus our Master has embraced us."

Isaiah 41:10 is posted on my computer at work so I see it every day and it says, "So do not fear, for I am with you; do not be dismayed, for I am your God. I will strengthen you and help you; I will uphold you with my righteous right hand."

I KNOW that God is upholding me, because I would not be here giving this message if He wasn't!

AJ's Story

My name is Shay Black. My son, AJ Black, died by suicide in his bedroom of our Johnstown home at 3a.m. on April first, 2016. AJ was 17 years old and a junior at Berthoud High School. He was gifted and talented in math and science, and in the STEM program. He was a wrestler, and even qualified and wrestled at state in the Pepsi Center in Denver in February of 2016. He loved to wrestle with his clubs and high school, wakeboard and camp at the lake, make music on his computer, do funny things with his friends, go shooting with his dad, and love on his yellow lab, Lacey. AJ had a great sense of humor, and was called the class clown on a daily basis. He could light up a room and turn the most serious conversation into fits of laughter. He certainly brightened our world, and it is dimmer now without him physically here beside us.

AJ was my only son. He was my baby, the youngest of three kids, with two older sisters. I will never forget seeing that ultrasound, and knowing that Alan and I would have a son. A son I could name after the love of my life. You see, Alan and I are your average everyday family. Married almost 28 years now, we started dating our senior year at Thompson Valley High School and got married two and a half years after graduation. Four years later, we welcomed

our first child, Rachel. Alisha came two years after that, and AJ came four years after that. Alan is an electrician and I work in oil and gas, and Alan is a native Northern Coloradoan. We have both coached youth sports in our community; Alan coached wrestling and I coached soccer. We enjoy summers at the lake on our boat and camping. We followed our kids in their endeavors from the girls' soccer, basketball and track to AJ's football, wrestling and robotics. We were your family next door, just like everyone else. And we were extremely blessed, as tragedy had not really ever directly hit our family. Of course, we had lost beloved grandparents, aunts and uncles, but most of our loss had followed the order of timing expected. We never thought something like losing our teenage son to suicide could happen to us. Until it did.

Why did AJ take his own life? The answer to that question is something that we may never know. He did not leave a note. He did not seem depressed. He was not on drugs or alcohol. He had his bags packed for a wrestling tournament trip and a turkey-hunting trip coming up in the days after his death. He even went online and worked on a homework project a little after 2 a.m. the morning he died. He was saving up for a watch, and had helped his dad pack his brand-new kayak into the trailer that was heading to the lake the next day. There was nothing on his phone or laptop that indicated anything. As parents, it feels like we have failed. Like one of the poems in AJ's memorial card said, "If only I had known it would be the last time I heard your voice, I would have kept you up just a little bit longer". But we didn't know. We had no way of knowing. Friends saw no signs, family saw no signs, school staff saw no signs, coaches saw no signs. Or were we just not educated? I can tell you that I do believe AJ was keeping something deep down inside of him that he felt was just too much for him to bear. For us to bear. For all of those who loved him to bear. And Satan lied to him and told him that we would all be better off without him here. He told him that he was a burden to his friends and family. He told him that we wouldn't miss him if he left. Society added to this by spreading stigma when it comes to mental health issues and suicide, making people like my son and so many others afraid and ashamed to speak out. These voices are nothing but lies, but when your mind is not functioning correctly, the voices seem to make sense. AJ's mind had been damaged by concussions and a society where social media can beat a kid down emotionally. His mental health failed him, and we failed to be educated on what could happen, because we never thought one of our kids could do something like this. We were wrong. And while I hate saying this, it needs to be said, anyone who thinks this could not possibly happen to their family is wrong. Satan and society are voicing evil into the heads of so many, most you would never even imagine are struggling.

We live in a world where we can order anything in mere seconds and have it delivered overnight express. We can access our family and friends in a click and post pictures of our lives right as we are living it. All without having face-to-face conversations. We are so used to just doing things without thinking, and unfortunately these snap decisions change way too many people's lives forever. The completion of suicide cannot be returned like a shirt ordered too small. Suicide has a permanent outcome. This world lost a great one the morning my son died, and our family lost a part of our hearts. We are one man down forever.

In the hours after AJ died, Alan and I were devastated. We knew what our faith was telling us, and we were trying our best to hang tightly to that. But in the dark of that first night without our son, it was just so much pain to endure. I confided in my husband that I was scared. I was scared because not only did I not know where my baby's body was, but I was worried about where his soul was. We prayed together, asking God to send us a tangible sign that AJ was okay. That AJ was in heaven. We spent a sleepless night, with night lights on, because the dark was just too dark. We listened to the hum of filter systems in AJ's bedroom, and we cried, prayed and held each other. The next day, I was contacted by a childhood friend from my days growing up back in Oklahoma. She had been living in Loveland for a long time (unknowingly to me), had seen on Facebook that our son had died, and wanted to bring food to us. I asked her to bring it to Alan's parent's house, as our family was all congregating over there. I told her that we would be in and out that day, and I couldn't promise I would be there. She said she was bringing food anyway. She showed up, and Alan and I just happened to be there. She asked me if I felt like I could tell her how AJ died. When I told her that he took his life, the shock on her face was quickly replaced with her realization that she had been sent to us for a purpose. See, both her parents had taken their own lives when she was younger. They were Christians, and she struggled with this, even to the point of lying to others about how they died, telling people they died in a car accident. The burden of where her parents had gone on to weighed heavy on her heart, and weighed down her young life. She strayed from the church, and made some choices that took her on a rough path. One day she finally came back around to her faith, and was shown a particular verse, John 10:28-29, "I give them eternal life, and they shall never perish; no one will snatch them out of my hand. My Father, who has given them to me, is greater than all; no one can snatch them out of my Father's hand." What this means is that once we are in His hands, our future is also in His hands. No one—NOT EVEN OURSELVES—can rob us of the certainty and security of eternal life. Once we have given our heart to Jesus, we may take our own physical life in our hands, but not our eternal life. Our eternal life is in His hands, not ours. My friend did not know how AJ died before coming over, and this scripture was in a sealed card that she gave me. She took my hands in her hands and told me that I have to let go of this burden of where my son is. Because he is with Jesus. He is safe. As I began to tell her the story of our time with AJ the night before, I mentioned that he had gone to his job at the pizza place that night. She stopped me and asked to see another picture of AJ, then proceeded to tell me that she and her husband had been served by AJ at the Brick Oven in Berthoud that very night. Not only had she been sent to me to comfort me, she saw my son the night he died. She said he was laughing and smiling, and cutting up with the other employees. In fact, she said they were laughing about one of them blowing up an onion in one of the ovens. I told her that sounded like something my class clown would have been involved in. Alan and I know in our hearts that this was our sign. And it amazingly confirmed what another dear friend had said to us the day before, "You don't get into heaven because of your actions, so you surely don't get turned away at the gate because of them." AJ is okay. AJ is safe. AJ is wrapped in God's love.

Since AJ's death, I have been so blessed by God through so many people sharing their hearts, but it is still so hard to contain so great an emptiness. My heart feels like it has been ripped out – it physically hurts inside my chest, my mind feels numb and many days it is hard to gather my thoughts, the sadness is so far reaching that it is indescribable. I have friends who have children in heaven, and I've always told Alan that if God took one of our kids before he took me, I wouldn't be able to bear it. But because of the amazing people I am surrounded by, I am consoled by my family and friends. I am comforted by messages and scripture. I am loved and held by my husband and daughters. I am carried by faith. And I see the hope in life daily.

But please understand, I am broken. Alan is broken. AJ's sisters are broken. Grandparents are broken. Teammates are broken. Coaches are broken. Friends and communities are broken. AJ made this choice himself, in the blink of an eye, and it was not the right choice. He saw no future, but he had a future. He saw no hope, but there was hope. I do believe that if AJ could change what happened and take it back, he would. His not yet fully developed and damaged mind could not rationalize the finality of this choice. So I now have a need to remind others the finality of it. This one decision ended his life here on earth. It is over. The harsh reality is, that AJ, and the many others who have made this decision, are not coming back. So many times, I read notes left by suicide victims stating that they were a burden, but that just was not true. The sad, and harsh, reality is that they actually become a burden to their families the moment their life ends. A burden that is so heavy to carry, but must be carried by suicide survivors for the rest of their lives.

I used to say that everything happened for a reason, and that everything that happens is God's plan, but I've changed. I have changed because I know in my heart that God's plan for my son was so much bigger than this. But God promised each of us a free will, and His promises endure. Could God have stopped AJ from dying that morning? Yes, but it was AJ's free will that made that decision and thwarted God's plans for his life. I think that as Christians, this is where we have to be very careful when dealing with mental health and suicide issues. Yes, because of our Faith, we know where AJ is at. He is in Heaven, and yes Heaven is a place beyond any wonderful place we can even imagine, but he should be here. He should not have gone into Heaven in the manner that he did. I understand that as pastors, caregivers, and support we have to uplift grieving families, friends, and communities and comfort them that their loved ones are safe in Heaven, but we also cannot stop the conversation there. We have to work with and be educated by mental health professionals on how to talk to others about mental health, how to throw out the stigma that comes with talking about it, and how to share with everyone that suicide is never the answer. It is not a way out of the pain here on earth. It simply shares that pain with family and friends. We have to show everyone that no matter how difficult this world is to live in, there is still life to live, many to love, and hope around each corner, but you have to keep walking forward to get around that corner. We do not want people who are struggling with mental health to see Heaven as the immediate way out and away from their pain. The only way to do that is to come together. Take the time to educate yourself now and in the days to come. Talk to others, and then walk out of here continuing the talk. Erase the stigma of talking about mental health and caring for others who are struggling with it. See mental health as the same thing as physical health. You would go to the doctor if you had a broken leg, because you know you need help to fix it. Your neighbors would come bring you food and help you to do tasks around your home, because they know you need it. Those struggling with mental health should be treated in the same exact way, because they also need it.

Visit with people at organizations like North Range Behavioral. Talk to them about the mental health education available and how you can help with the movement to replace stigma with love, openness, acceptance and hope. Mental health first aid is an 8-hour class that I encourage everyone to take. The Youth Mental Health 1st Aid class through North Range Behavioral in Greeley, Colorado is eye opening, and I feel should be mandatory, for those of us who work with youth. And it's free. Reaching out is the most important thing to continue.

Suicide survivors find themselves on a road they never wanted to travel, but are forced to. It is a sad, long, bumpy road with way too many others who were already on it, and way too many who join you along the way. Most of the parents on this road have kids just like mine; normal, physically healthy, active, funny, loving kids – kids who nobody ever expected this from. Many of us, like Alan and I, don't get typical warning signs. We just get blindsided, and then we search for answers. It is these things that have caused Alan and I to start a 501c3 non-profit organization called The AJ Black Foundation. Our goal is to work with our local mental health professionals to get mental health education and suicide awareness into our schools, clubs, churches, and communities. We also understand how important post-vention is when a suicide happens, and we are working with local support groups and first responders to get Care Kits into the hands of parents who lose a child by suicide right when it happens. Our Care Kits simply contain things that brought us comfort in the days after AJ died. We were surrounded by so much support and love, but it opened our eyes and made us question how families new to town or a single parent copes. Suicide is a trauma that there are no words for, and the pain doesn't end on the day that life ends, or the day of the funeral, or even a year after. The pain never ends for suicide survivors.

To all those struggling: please don't let this happen to your mom, your dad, your grandparents, your friends. Don't leave them here crying, sick with heartache. Don't bottle up the feelings you have, pushing them deep down inside. Don't think that there is anything in this world that you can do or say that will make your parents not love you. Their love is unconditional. There will certainly be discipline and teaching, because that is what a parent does, but their love will go on forever and through anything. Reach out to each other. Keep tabs on each other. Check in with each other. Don't assume that your friends know you love them. Tell them and tell them often. Pull together and pull each other through the darkness. Let go of the stigma associated with talking about suicide, or the worry of what people will think if you ask for help. We all have issues and struggle with stress. All of us.

My son was a loving kid. I have so many messages from his friends telling me stories about times AJ was kind to them, made them laugh, made them smile, and pulled them out of a dreary day. I just wish he would have been able to do that for himself in that short moment, and see the value in himself that he obviously saw in others. Sometimes the ones we all think are doing the best and are always happy and well adjusted, are the ones who need our help the most. Many times they are the ones who push the hurt and sadness so deep, and then cover it so well. Parents, keep tabs on your kids, what they are doing and who they are with. Know their friends; check their cell phones and computers. Make sure they know that you are on their side and will support them through anything. And then know that sometimes none of it is enough. So you have to reach out for help as well. Do not ever be ashamed to do this. Reach out, always reach out. Continue to do this for your kids, for your family, for yourself.

nineteen

HOPE FOR THE STRUGGLING ONES

THERE ARE, OF COURSE, NO EASY ANswers for people who may be struggling with mental health issues. Those of you who want to help your friend or loved one find solutions know how difficult that can be.

Talk to your primary-care doctor or another health professional about mental health problems. Ask them to connect you with the right mental health services. You may also find answers at MentalHealth.gov.

If you or someone you know is struggling with suicidal thoughts, contact:

National Suicide Prevention Lifeline: 1-800-273-TALK (8255) or suicidepreventionlifeline.org

National Hopeline Network: 1-800-SUICIDE (784-2433) or hopeline.com

Crisis Text Line: text HELP to 741741

Colorado Crisis Services: 1-844-493-TALK (8255) or text TALK to 38255

Safe2tell Colorado: 1-877-542-7233 or safe2tell.org

Safe2tell is a safe, anonymous way to help someone who is struggling or hurting. They help you learn what to look for, what to listen for and what to report.

Veterans Crisis Line: 1-800-273-8255, text 838255, or veteranscrisisline.net

If you have lost someone to suicide, learn more about support groups and resources available to you by visiting allianceforsuicideprevention.org.

Another very helpful website is the American Foundation for Suicide Prevention, afsp.org. The Foundation raises awareness, funds scientific research and provides resources and aid to those affected by suicide. It funds research to improve interventions, trains clinicians in suicide prevention, and advocates for policy that will save lives.

AJ Black Foundation

A non-profit organization dedicated to suicide awareness and prevention through improving mental health awareness and education in our schools and throughout our community, as well as offering support of families immediately after a suicide with distribution of care kits. Website: www.ajblackfoundation.org

J.O.S.H.

A non-profit organization that provides an environment where kids can develop confidence, self-esteem and optimism for a bright future.  Members of the program know they belong and feel valued by one another and that their lives matter. Run by the Berthoud Athletic Club. Follow on Facebook: J.O.S.H. Journey of Strength and Hope

3 Hopeful Hearts is dedicated to helping provide parents and families with support after the loss of a child. Visit their website: 3hopefulhearts.com

twenty

FOUR-LEGGED COMFORT AND HOPE

W E WALKED INTO THE LIBRARY OF Windsor High School. The atmosphere hung heavy; the snow clouds of that December day seemed to hang in the hallways of the school. As part of the LCC K-9 Comfort Dog Team, we were invited by one of the teachers and several school counselors to bring Cubby to provide some peaceful compassion. The three of us were ushered into a smaller meeting room off the library. We sat on the floor awaiting some of the students. Cubby looked at us with wondering eyes. "What can we do for these grieving students?" she seemed to be asking. As they arrived with their heads down, tear-streaked faces revealing their emotional status, Cubby knew. "Just be there. Let them pet my soft, warm fur. Pray with them. Hug them. Allow them to cry." Or even scream, as one young student did, out of shock and sheer desperation.

These vulnerable, innocent young people, most of whom had never experienced tragedies or even the death of a loved one, were thrown into the reality of the end of life: one of their own. It brought to the forefront how precious life is and that death, even suicide, can happen to someone their own age.

Cubby's calming demeanor comforted some students that day. Cubby had offered that same comfort the month before to students and faculty at Berthoud High School, where a student had taken his own life. She brought Jesus's compassion to that same student's memorial service and gave the family, especially the young children, hugging time and an outlet for the tears to flow.

The LCC K-9 Comfort Dog Ministry is a national ministry that utilizes the unique traits of dogs, specifically golden retrievers, to open opportunities to touch people with mercy and compassion. The dogs are trained for over 2,000 hours and prepared to interact with people in ways that provide a bridge for compassionate ministry to take place.

LCC K-9 Comfort Dogs bring comfort to individuals and families who are suffering pain or loss. They calm individuals, facilitate conversation, work with special-needs individuals, veterans, and the elderly, and are used in counseling situations. The dogs also respond to crisis and disaster situations for the entire nation.

In Colorado, Cubby the K-9 Comfort Dog responds to crisis and counseling situations and is available to provide comfort when needed. Her contact information is:

Cubby@K9Comfort.org, or redeemerconnect.com, or 970-225-9020.

For the national LCC K-9 Comfort Dog Ministry, contact: K9Comfort.org

Proceeds from the sale of this book will go toward this organization to benefit those who have been affected by suicide. To learn more about this organization contact:

Making A Difference
(866) 455-6466
3020 Milwaukee Ave
Northbrook, Illinois 60062
LCC@LutheranChurchCharities.org

The following literature can be helpful.

From "Dealing with Suicide & Depression in Teen Literature" on the Young Adult Library Services Association website.

Gayle Forman, *I Was Here* (New York: Penguin Random House, 2016)

Cynthia Hand, *The Last Time We Say Goodbye* (New York: Harper Teen, 2015)

Jennifer Niven, *All the Bright Places* (New Zealand: Random House Children's Books, 2015)

Andrew Slaby and Lili Frank Garfinkle, *No One Saw My Pain: Why Teens Kill Themselves* (New York: W.W. Norton and Company, 1996)

Jasmine Warga, *My Heart and Other Black Holes* (New York: Harper Collins/Balzar & Bray, 2015)

Books for adults dealing with grief after losing a loved one to suicide:

Bob Baugher, Ph.D. and Jack Jorday, Ph.D., *After Suicide Loss: Coping with Your Grief* (Branson: Caring People Press, 2016)

Jane Butler, *A Force Unfamiliar to Me: A Cautionary Tale* (Hamlet Books, 1998)

Beverly Cobain and Jean Larch, *Dying to Be Free* (Center City: Hazelden Foundation, 2006)

Judy Collins, *Sanity and Grace: A Journey of Suicide, Survival, and Strength* (New York: Tarcher/Penguin, 2003)

Eric Hipple with Dr. Gloria Horsley and Dr. Heidi Horsley, *Real Men Do Cry: A Quarterback's Inspiring Story of Tackling Depression and Surviving Suicide Loss* (Naples: Quality of Life Publishing Co., 2008)

Linda H. Kilburn, M.S.W., *Reaching Out After Suicide: What's Helpful and What's Not* (Available from KP Associates, LLC (KPAMASS@ aol.com) 2008)

Christopher Lukas and Henry Selden, *Silent Grief: Living in the Wake of Suicide* (London: Jessica Kingsley Publishers, 2007)

Michael F. Myers, M.D. and Carla Fine, *Touched by Suicide: Hope and Healing after Loss* (New York: Gotham Books, 2006)

Ann Smolin and John Guinan, *Healing After the Suicide of a Loved One* (New York: Fireside Books/Simon and Schuster, 1993)

Alan D. Wolfelt, PhD., *Understanding Your Suicide Grief* (Fort Collins: Companion Press, 2009)

Adina Wrobleski, *Suicide of a Child* (Omaha: Centering Corp., 1993)